The Harvey Milk Story

by
Kari Krakow

illustrated by
David C. Gardner

Lee & Low Books Inc.
New York

For Peter, Hattie and Willa.
—K.K.

To Mark and my mother and father. For all of us.
—D.C.G.

LEE & LOW BOOKS Inc., 95 Madison Avenue, New York, NY 10016
leeandlow.com

Book design by Elliane Mellet • Book production by The Kids at Our House
The text is set in Quicksand. • Manufactured in South Korea by Mirae-N
10 9 8 7 6 5 4 3 2 1
Second Edition

Library of Congress Cataloging-in-Publication Data
Names: Krakow, Kari, author. | Gardner, David (David Colby), 1959- illustrator.
Title: The Harvey Milk story / by Kari Krakow ; illustrated by David C. Gardner.
Description: Second Edition. | New York : Lee & Low Books Inc., 2022. |
First edition: 2001. | Includes bibliographical references. | Audience:
Ages 6-8 years | Audience: Grades 2-3 | Summary: "Picture book biography
of Harvey Milk, one of the first openly gay elected officials in the U.S"--
Provided by publisher. • Identifiers: LCCN 2021054400 |
ISBN 9781643796000 (Paperback) | ISBN 9781643796017 (eBook)
Subjects: LCSH: Milk, Harvey--Juvenile literature. |
Politicians--California--San Francisco--Biography--Juvenile literature.
| Gay politicians--California--San Francisco--Biography--Juvenile
literature. | San Francisco (Calif.)--Politics and government--
20th century--Juvenile literature. | San Francisco
(Calif.)--Biography--Juvenile literature. | Gay liberation
movement--California--San Francisco--History--
20th century--Juvenile literature.
Classification: LCC F869.S353 M546
2022 | DDC 979.4/61053092 [B]--
dc23/eng/20211206
LC record available at
https://lccn.loc.gov/2021054400

"The only thing they have to look
forward to is hope. And you have to
give them hope. Hope for a better world,
hope for a better tomorrow . . .
hope that all will be all right."

—HARVEY MILK

No one would have ever guessed that the little kid with big ears would one day make history. Harvey Bernard Milk was born the second son of a middle-class Jewish family on May 22, 1930. He grew up in Woodmere, New York.

As a child, Harvey loved to be the center of attention. On Saturday afternoons, he would delight his family by pretending to conduct the unseen orchestra blaring from the radio on the mantel.

Minnie Milk was especially proud of her intelligent and energetic son. She recognized in him an independent spirit and encouraged him to stand up for what he believed in. Harvey never forgot the day his mother told him about the brave Jews of the Warsaw Ghetto, who continued to defend themselves even when outnumbered and surrounded by Nazis.

Harvey loved sports. His height made him a natural on the basketball team, and he participated in track and wrestling. He also played linebacker for Bayshore High's football team, wearing jersey number 60.

Harvey was always popular. It was hard to find anyone who wasn't his friend. Always ready with a joke and a smile, he knew how to make people laugh. He had something special that years later politicians would call charisma. Everyone knew Harvey and liked him.

What his friends and family didn't know was that Harvey was growing up gay. Harvey knew he was gay by the time he was fourteen, but he would keep that part of himself a closely guarded secret for many years to come. Like so many people of his time, he was afraid of what would happen to him if others knew he was gay. Fears that he would be beaten up at school and abandoned by his friends and family troubled his sleep and tormented his days.

A good student, Harvey finished high school a year early and went on to the New York State College for Teachers. He continued playing football and basketball and was the sports editor for the *State College News* in his senior year. Harvey was handed his college diploma on a warm day in June 1951, while his parents proudly looked on.

After college, Harvey joined the Navy. He became an expert deep-sea diver and taught others to maneuver heavy equipment on the ocean floor. Rising rapidly through the ranks, Harvey soon became chief petty officer on the USS *Kittiwake*, a submarine rescue vessel that cruised the Pacific. When he went to his brother Robert's wedding, he looked so handsome in his Navy uniform that his family and friends all wondered when he would settle down and get married to the "right girl."

Harvey did fall in love and settle down. But the right person was a handsome young man named Joe Campbell. They moved together to Rego Park, New York, where Harvey taught math and science at Hewlett High School and coached basketball after school. They were happy together, but Harvey kept their relationship a secret. Harvey feared he would lose his job, his friends, and his family if people found out he was gay. Keeping such a big part of their lives secret put a lot of stress on Harvey and Joe's relationship, and after six years they separated.

Harvey was tired of hiding the fact that he was gay. So when he met and fell in love with Scott Smith, they moved together to a neighborhood in San Francisco known as the Castro. The Castro was becoming a gay neighborhood, a place where a gay couple could walk down the street, hold hands, and show all the signs of affection, joy, and pride that people do when they are in love.

Harvey and Scott put their money together and invested in camera supplies and a five-year lease for a Victorian storefront on Castro Street. They moved in upstairs and opened Castro Camera on the first floor. For the first time in his life, Harvey felt like he could finally be himself.

Harvey took time to talk to his customers, and he was always ready to help or offer advice. New Castro residents came by to ask where to look for an apartment or how to find that first job. The store's large picture windows displayed announcements, petitions, and notices of neighborhood meetings. Castro Camera quickly became a community center.

As Harvey listened to people, he realized that the Castro community needed a leader. Gay people had no legal protections, and they risked losing their jobs and homes. They were harassed by the police. To help change laws and fight for the rights of gay people, Harvey decided to run for public office in San Francisco.

Many people wanted to help elect Harvey Milk. They liked him and his ideas. Friends, neighbors, and customers volunteered their time to send out mailings, paint posters, and answer phones. Eleven-year-old Medora Payne came every day after school to lick envelopes and hand out brochures for Harvey. She organized a fundraiser at her school, earning $39.28 for his campaign.

Some people thought that the Harvey Milk campaign was a joke. They thought it was impossible for an openly gay candidate to get elected in San Francisco, because none had before. Harvey ran for public office three times between 1973 and 1976. Each time he lost.

But Harvey didn't lose hope or give up. He knew that having an openly gay leader at City Hall would give people the courage to be proud of who they were. He kept on trying, and each time he ran for office he came closer to winning. He worked tirelessly, talking to the people in his district. Harvey showed respect for the diverse cultures of his community. He spoke out for the rights of people who were often ignored by the city government: African Americans, Asian Americans, senior citizens, people with disabilities, and gays and lesbians.

More and more people began to agree with his ideas about fairness and justice. They sensed that Harvey would stand up for what he believed in and make a difference in city government. In 1977, he ran again for San Francisco's Board of Supervisors, and this time he won. On a rainy day in January, on the steps of San Francisco's City Hall, Harvey Milk became the first openly gay man sworn in to public office in the United States of America. Harvey Milk had made history.

As a supervisor, Harvey Milk got to work on the issues that the people of San Francisco cared about: schools, parks, police protection, and housing. He helped make laws to ensure the quality of life for all people. After fighting against the closing of a neighborhood school, he said, "Our cities must not be abandoned. They're worth fighting for, not just by those who live in them, but by industry, commerce, unions, everyone. What we need is a neighborhood where people can walk to work, raise their kids, enjoy life. That simple."

Supervisor Milk fought hard to introduce a gay rights bill for San Francisco. This law would protect gay people from discrimination at work and when choosing a home. Ten of the eleven supervisors on the city council voted for the gay rights bill, and San Francisco's mayor, George Moscone, enthusiastically signed the bill into law. "I don't do this enough," said the mayor, "taking swift and unambiguous action on a substantial move for civil rights."

The gay people of San Francisco were now legally protected from being harassed at their workplaces and losing their jobs and homes. More and more gay people were able to come out of hiding and live in the open. In the 1978 Gay Freedom Day Parade, nearly four hundred thousand people marched through downtown San Francisco. Harvey Milk proudly rode at the center of the parade as thousands cheered.

That day Harvey Milk gave a speech to the huge mass of people that had settled in front of City Hall. He called for a Gay Rights March in Washington, DC, to show the nation that gay people would no longer hide. Harvey Milk was a hero.

But some people felt threatened by the growing gay movement. They hated and feared the idea of gay people having the same rights as everyone else. Dan White was one of those people. He was the only supervisor to vote against the gay rights bill. He tried to prevent the San Francisco Gay Freedom Parade from taking place. He was voted down.

Dan White didn't like to lose. He was so frustrated by his lack of power and so jealous of Harvey Milk's growing popularity that he resigned from the Board of Supervisors. Ten days later, he changed his mind and asked to be reappointed. When Mayor Moscone would not give him his job back, he was angry.

On a gray November morning, Dan White crawled through a basement window at the back of City Hall with a loaded gun.

Dan White entered the mayor's office and, after a brief argument took place, shot Mayor George Moscone. Reloading his gun, he hurried down the hall to Harvey Milk's office. Five shots rang out.

Both Mayor Moscone and Harvey Milk were killed.

People everywhere were stunned by the news of the double assassination. They left their homes, jobs, and schools to mourn the loss of these two great leaders. Crowds began forming in front of City Hall. By nightfall thousands filled the mile-long street that ran from the Castro to City Hall. They stood in silence, carrying candles. That night the people of San Francisco wept.

Harvey Milk was gone, but his dream lived on. The next October, 1979, over one hundred thousand people responded to his call. They participated in the first Gay Rights March in Washington, DC, and thousands carried portraits in memory of the slain leader. Harvey Milk would not be forgotten.

Epilogue

Harvey Milk's memory continues to live on in many places and in many ways. His life has been the subject of books, plays, films, and even an opera. In San Francisco, the Harvey Milk Memorial Plaza marks the entrance to the Castro, and a statue of him now stands in the rotunda in City Hall. Government buildings and schools around the world bear his name, including the Castro elementary school that Harvey fought to keep open, the Harvey Milk Civil Rights Academy. Harvey Milk posthumously received the Medal of Freedom in 2009 from President Barack Obama. He was also inducted into the California Hall of Fame, and his birthday, May 22, is now celebrated annually in the state and elsewhere as Harvey Milk Day. In 2014, he became the first openly gay public official to appear on a US postage stamp, and in 2021, the US Navy named a ship after him, the USNS *Harvey Milk*. For more information about Harvey and the ongoing work in his name toward education and equality, visit the Harvey Milk Foundation website at milkfoundation.org.

Harvey Milk believed that one person could make a difference in the lives of others. His legacy continues to inspire and give people hope as they struggle for justice. Nearly half of all cities and states now have laws prohibiting discrimination against lesbian, gay, bisexual, transgender, and queer (LGBTQ) people in employment and housing. In 2015, the Supreme Court decided that that all states must recognize same-sex marriages. More and more LGBTQ people are running for office and getting elected. While more remains to be done, Harvey Milk once said, "The true function of politics is not just to pass laws, but to give hope." Harvey Milk pioneered a road to freedom. He showed the world that all people can have their hopes realized.

Author's Notes

p. 6: "Harvey never forgot . . . the brave Jews of the Warsaw Ghetto, who continued to defend themselves even when outnumbered and surrounded by Nazis."

In 1940, the Jewish residents of Warsaw, Poland were forced into an area known as a "ghetto," which was sealed off by a ten-foot wall and guarded by Nazi troops. Thousands of people died from starvation, disease, and cold. In 1942, three hundred thousand Jews were deported to the Treblinka extermination camp. When reports of mass killings in Treblinka leaked back to the ghetto, the surviving Jews organized a rebellion. They refused to report for deportation and bravely battled the Nazis against incredible odds. After days of fighting, the Nazi troops retreated. Even though the Nazis later destroyed the ghetto, this struggle inspired resistance groups throughout Europe to fight against Nazi oppression.

p. 9: "Fears that he would be beaten up at school and abandoned by his friends and family troubled his sleep and tormented his days."

When Harvey was young, most LGBTQ people were forced to keep their lives a secret. They were misrepresented and misunderstood. Even friends and family members might reject someone if they found out he, she, or they had a different sexual or gender identity. Harvey Milk gave many people the courage to live openly despite the risks.

Today most people know someone who is LGBTQ. More and more LGBTQ people live proudly as who they are and are acknowledged for the important contributions they make to our society. Harvey Milk believed that one person could make a difference in the lives of others.

Each of us, straight and LGBTQ, can make a difference too. We can respect and value the LGBTQ people in our lives and encourage our schools and communities to be safe and welcoming places for all. If you feel you might be LGBTQ yourself, you can visit the Trevor Project at thetrevorproject.org to get more information and find support. For more information about creating supportive school communities, check out the Gay, Lesbian and Straight Education Network at glsen.org. To support LGBTQ family and friends, contact PFLAG (formerly Parents, Families, and Friends of Lesbians and Gays) at pflag.org.

p. 16: "Gay people had no legal protections, and they risked losing their jobs and homes."

When Harvey Milk was a young man, overt discrimination against groups of people was legal and commonplace. African American people were denied equal access to public places. Jewish people were barred from membership in clubs and organizations. Women were not allowed entry to many universities. LGBTQ people were also the subject of prejudice and mistreatment. They could be harassed, arrested, and sometimes beaten by police for going to gay bars or clubs. Violence against LGBTQ people was ignored by law enforcement and the legal system. Gays and lesbians were routinely fired from their jobs and evicted from their homes. For these reasons, they were often forced to hide their identities and relationships. Many people fought to create laws that protect against discrimination. Harvey Milk was one of them.

The fight continues. In 2020, the Supreme Court ruled that employers cannot discriminate against LGBTQ Americans. Cities and towns across the country have adopted civil rights ordinances to help ensure that LGBTQ people receive fair treatment. But many other cities and towns have not, meaning that legal protections for LGBTQ people often depend on where they live in the United States. Transgender people especially struggle to have their rights and identities recognized. For more information about laws protecting LGBTQ people, visit the Lambda Legal Defense and Education Fund at lambdalegal.org.

p. 20: "Harvey Milk became the first openly gay man sworn in to public office in the United States."

Harvey Milk was not the first openly LGBTQ person elected in the US. In 1974, Kathy Kozachenko won a city council race in Ann Arbor, Michigan. Later that year, Elaine Noble took a seat in the Massachusetts General Assembly—the first LGBTQ person elected to statewide office.

Bibliography

Books

Marcus, Eric. *Making History: The Struggle for Gay and Lesbian Equal Rights*. New York: HarperCollins, 1992.

Miller, Neil. *Out of the Past: Gay and Lesbian History from 1869 to the Present*. New York: Vintage Books, 1995.

Shilts, Randy. *The Mayor of Castro Street: The Life and Times of Harvey Milk*. New York: St. Martin's Press, 1982.

Films

Epstein, Rob, dir. *The Times of Harvey Milk*. San Francisco,: Black Sands Productions, 1984.

Stein, Peter, dir. *The Castro*. San Francisco: KQED, 1997.

Periodicals

The Advocate, 1977-1979.

The San Francisco Chronicle, 1977-1979.

The San Francisco Examiner, 1977-1979.

More Resources on LGBTQ History

Picture Books

Ellison, Joy Michael. *Sylvia and Marsha Start a Revolution!: The Story of the Trans Women of Color Who Made LGBTQ+ History*. Philadelphia: Jessica Kingsley Publishers, 2020.

Pitman, Gayle E. *Sewing the Rainbow: A Story About Gilbert Baker*. Washington, DC: Magination Press, 2020.

Sanders, Rob. *Pride: The Story of Harvey Milk and the Rainbow Flag*. New York: Random House Books for Young Readers, 2018.

Sanders, Rob. *Stonewall: A Building. An Uprising. A Revolution*. New York: Random House Books for Young Readers, 2019.

Middle Grade & Young Adult

Bronski, Michael. *A Queer History of the United States for Young People*. ReVisioning History for Young People. Adapted by Richie Chevat. Boston: Beacon Press, 2019.

Prager, Sarah. *Rainbow Revolutionaries: Fifty LGBTQ+ People Who Made History*. New York: HarperCollins, 2020.

Sicardi, Arabelle. *Queer Heroes: Meet 53 LGBTQ Heroes From Past and Present!* London: Wide Eyed Editions, 2019.

Adult

Faderman, Lillian. *Harvey Milk: His Lives and Death*. Jewish Lives. New Haven: Yale University Press, 2019.

Milk, Harvey. *An Archive of Hope: Harvey Milk's Speeches and Writings*. Edited by Jason Edward Black and Charles E. Morris. Berkeley: University of California Press, 2013.

Reynolds, Andrew. *The Children of Harvey Milk: How LGBTQ Politicians Changed the World*. New York: Oxford University Press, 2018.

Film

Van Sant, Gus, dir. *Milk*. Universal City, CA: Focus Features, 2009.